PAWS 4 PEACE

*Enhancing Restorative Practices
with Therapy Dogs*

by Patricia E. LaTaille

PAWS 4 PEACE
Enhancing Restorative Practices
with Therapy Dogs
by: Patricia E. LaTaille

Cover image credit: Molly Rowan Leach

Copyright 2018

ISBN 978-1-7336265-0-7
Library of Congress
Control Number 2019900516

writewithlightpublications.com

"Because of the dog's joyfulness, our own is increased. It is no small gift. It is not the least reason why we should honor as well as love the dog of our own life, and the dog down the street, and all the dogs not yet born."
Mary Oliver (American Poet)

Dedication

To our Therapy Dogs who demonstrate unconditional love and canine compassion, together with their humans, who bring peace and comfort to those in need.

FCRJ Paws 4 Peace Parade, Salida, 2017

Acknowledgments

With great gratitude to our pioneering Therapy Dog Teams who enhance Restorative Justice Practices; 'Abby' with Ruth and Greg Phillips, 'Dolores' with Terry and Gary Bolte, 'Keet' with Paula and Bryan Barclay, 'Ringo' with Sue Armijo, and 'Rosie' and 'Emma' with Debby Gower.

Special thanks to Peter Simonson, Past President of the Full Circle Restorative Justice (FCRJ) Board of Directors, former and current FCRJ staff members & dog lovers: Dianne Walker, Jenn Ricci, Ange Welborn, Andrea Blocker, Jessica Ervin, Sarah Green, Molly Rohan Leach, Stephanie Jones, J.D. Longwell and the FCRJ "Powerhouse of Volunteers"; with past and current members of the Board of Directors, and all of our FCRJ Family of Facilitators.

Muchas Gracias a mi amigo Diego Rojas Lopez por su patiencia y por sus habilidades con el teclado.

Lots of puppy kisses and doggy love to our dear friends and colleagues at the Chaffee County Courthouse, especially "Aunties" Becky, Teresa, Terry, Steph, and Jazz.

Many thanks to Peter Holt for his exacting and thorough editing skills, coupled with a charming Canadian accent.

Heaps of love and peace to my supportive soul sister and brother Phoebe & Andrew Crane and their animal menagerie Down Under.

Forever in gratitude to my father George J. Lataille for his unwavering support and love throughout all of my escapades.

With deep appreciation for Kathleen Kennedy from Write With Light Publications for her support and enthusiasm.

Most of all, I offer love and appreciation to Kharmalita, Maya, Ponyboy, Tari, Cheeto, Cinder, Geeba, Matchka, and all of the animals that have enhanced my life and brought joy to friends and family.

Paws and Peace to all,

Patty LaTaille
San Miguel de Allende, GTO. Mexico, May 2018
Salida, Colorado USA, February 2019

Foreword

"Petting, scratching and cuddling a dog could be as soothing to the mind and heart as deep meditation -and almost as good for the soul as prayer."
Dean R. Koontz, American Author

Bringing people together in a Restorative Justice (RJ) Circle means bringing someone who has created harm together with the victim of his/her offense, in addition to family members and community members. The Circle can be a very powerful and healing space, but it also can initially be a very uncomfortable and difficult space to be a part of.

Imagine sitting in a circle, face to face, with the person who has harmed you.

Or, maybe, you are the individual who has harmed someone else.

Would you both feel nervous, anxious, sad, and upset?

As RJ facilitators, we have seen all of these emotions and many more. It is part of our job to create a safe and supportive environment for all. **The use of Therapy Dogs in RJ is beautiful!**

Research has shown the therapeutic value of pets for those who have experienced difficulties and trauma in their lives. It is our hope and wish that Restorative Justice Practitioners around the globe will understand and consider the therapeutic value of utilizing therapy dogs in their restorative practices. It is an opportunity to provide another level of healing and care for those we work with.

***Paws 4 Peace* – Enhancing Restorative Practices with Therapy Dogs is the handbook to help make this happen!**

A special "thanks" to Patty LaTaille for all of the work and outreach she has done in bringing therapy dogs into restorative practices.

With much appreciation,
Colorado State Senator Pete Lee (D)
RJ Practitioner, Trainer, and RJ CO State Council member Lynn Lee

*"All dogs are therapy dogs
The majority of them are just freelancing."*
Author Unknown

**National Association of Community and Restorative Justice Conference
Oakland California June 2016**

Karen Lee, Lynn & Senator Pete Lee, Greg & Ruth Phillips,
Patty LaTaille and Abby

Chapter 1

The Power of Paws

"A dog judges others not by their color or creed or class, but by who they are inside. A dog doesn't care if you are rich or poor, educated or illiterate, clever or dull. Give him your heart and he will give you his." John Grogan (Author, Marley & Me)

This book is written to inspire and encourage fellow Restorative Justice (RJ) Facilitators, and to all of the dedicated individuals involved in this critical social justice work, both Human and Canine alike. My hope is that RJ practitioners will consider enhancing restorative practices in their communities by inviting Therapy Dog teams into school programs, the Courts and Restorative Circles/Victim-Offender (V-O) conferences.

Many individuals wonder what exactly Restorative Justice is, (other than what may be initially considered an oxymoron). So let us begin with describing RJ in the quintessential two minutes or less 'Elevator Speech':

Restorative Justice is an evidence-based peace-building conflict resolution process. It involves a common sense approach to dealing with incidents of crime and/or conflict by addressing the needs of victims within a community-centered approach to resolving issues and repairing harm.

Two parties, (the individuals responsible for and those impacted by a crime or conflict, together with each party's personal family/support people), meet with trained facilitators who initiate, guide, and engage the participants in dialogue within a Restorative Circle. These individuals, supported by community members, meet face-to-face while a Therapy Dog Team assists them in smoothing the way for an often emotional process, which holds offenders accountable and develops an agreement to repair the harm caused.

RJ is unique in its focus on the "back story", its compassionate approach of respecting all participants equally, and in providing the means to "make it right", which leads to healing and a sense of closure for, both, victims and offenders. RJ is also based on the idea of interrelationships, which are affected by harm done, and the obligations that arise from this, as well as requiring the participation and engagement of all of the stakeholders involved.

"Crime represents damaged relationships," offers Howard Zehr, one of the founders of the RJ movement in the United States and author of *The Little Book of Restorative Justice*. Zehr is considered the "Grandfather of modern day RJ". His book emphasizes identifying the justice needs of everyone involved in a crime. This has become a worldwide movement of growing influence that is helping victims and communities heal, while holding offenders accountable for their actions.

Zehr explains in his *Little Book of RJ*:
"Although the term 'restorative justice' encompasses a variety of programs and practices at its core, it is a set of principles and values, of philosophy, and an alternate set of guiding questions. Ultimately, restorative justice provides an alternative framework for thinking about wrongdoing.

'Restorative Practices' include positive non-punitive approaches to repairing the harm caused by criminal offenses which affect victims and the community. These practices include Victim-Offender conferences (RJ Circles), school truancy and discipline-related conferences with a victim-centered approach to community justice and conflict resolution."

RJ offers a paradigm shift in thinking about how justice is traditionally served. We move from "Offense & Offender-based" to "Victim-Centered" Justice with individuals known as "the person harmed" (Victim) and "the person who caused harm" (Offender).

Zehr shares that, "Many feel that the criminal justice process deepens societal wounds and conflicts rather that contributing to healing or peace." This is evidenced in the different approaches towards addressing crime and justice:

The traditional systems of justice asks: 1. *What laws have been broken? 2. Who did it? 3. What do they deserve?*
Restorative Justice asks: *1. Who has been hurt? 2. What are their needs? 3. Who is responsible for meeting these needs?*

This holistic approach to dealing with crime and conflict offers us a way to "humanize" our overloaded and imperfect system of justice. Justice does not always mean punishment.

RJ also gives offenders a chance to move past any shame associated with their actions and provides the opportunity to rebuild relationships and reputations. (This is HUGE in reducing recidivism in youth!)

Inviting in a therapy dog to help shift and stabilize the Circle's energy, provides willing participants a warmer and more connective RJ process - complete with canines.

Daniel Hufford with Abby, 2017

Patty LaTaille

As the former Executive Director and current Program Director over a span of thirteen years at Full Circle Restorative Justice (FCRJ) in Salida, Colorado, I am overwhelmingly grateful to an exceptional group of dedicated volunteers who are always willing to try new ideas and practices. These individuals were more than willing to pioneer the approach of inviting Therapy Dog Teams into the victim-offender conferencing process.

The idea of dogs in Circles germinated during a training in which while I invited our veteran RJ facilitators to think about and to describe what was the most awkward and uncomfortable moments in the RJ process for the facilitators and participants.

Invariably, the answer was that the most excruciating time is the initial few minutes of the process when the "Victims" and "Offenders" first meet each other in what is known as the Restorative Circle (or the Victim-Offender Dialogue - VOD). This valuable insight is important, because the initial meeting of the victim and offender can set the tone for the conference.

As an experienced facilitator, I mulled over how to ease the inherent tension and desired to have an ice-breaker to assist in creating connection and building rapport. Who better to do this than a docile dog – a cute canine connector who can meet the needs for ease and comfort?

I glanced over at my little dog "Kharmie", sleeping peacefully on her bed after greeting all of her FCRJ family and friends. A quote by Edith Wharton; "My little dog – a heartbeat at my feet"; always surfaced in my mind when I had her with me. The pleasure that accompanied Kharmie's appearance in the FCRJ office and trainings was palpable. Would it be possible to bring well-trained dogs into RJ and let them work their magic to reduce the inherent tension between Victims and Offenders?

As it turns out, it was not only possible – it was a miraculously "pawsitive". (As *Susan Ariel Rainbow Kennedy noted; "Dogs are miracles with paws!"*) FCRJ results are conclusive: introducing therapy dogs appears to enhance the RJ process for the majority of Circle participants.

The canines in question are specially trained, and then certified - mainly by the National Alliance of Therapy Dogs and/or other certifying agencies - and are teamed up with their human handlers who are RJ trained and certified facilitators. By inviting a therapy dog into the Circle, significant steps are in place to help ease the tension and calm the anxiety experienced by participants. The therapy dog team also attends the initial Pre-conferences (precursors to the Circle) and ideally are in the courtroom when the individual cases from the judge, district attorney, public defender and/or probation officer, etc. are referred.

The use of therapy dogs is constantly expanding as an increasing number of individuals and institutions, such as schools, libraries, hospitals, hospice, nursing homes, airports, medical research studies, retirement homes, veteran rehab centers, search and rescue efforts, Restorative Justice programs, etc. are now recognizing the importance of the Human-Animal Bond. Therapy dogs illustrate how this bond benefits individuals, and enhances the therapeutic and legal processes taking place.

"The impact of using a therapy dog in restorative justice circles became clear during the very first Circle Abby was involved in. Both the offender and his mother had been previously diagnosed with anxiety disorders and were extremely stressed about the Circle. While they shared their story, Abby sat between them. As they spoke, they gently stroked Abby. Both commented later how Abby's presence helped get them through a very difficult experience."

-- Shared by Ruth Phillips, with Abby – FCRJ Therapy Dog Team

"I have found that when you are deeply troubled, there are things you get from the silent devoted companionship of a dog that you can get from no other source." – Doris Day (American Actor)

FCRJ Past Board President Peter Simonson
and our "Mascot" Kharmie, 2017

Chapter 2

Paws 4 Peace Program

"Therapy dogs visit people in nursing homes, hospitals, and wherever else they are needed. They cheer people up who are sad or lonesome, and just need a furry friend to hug."
— Martha McKiever *(Author, Finn's Trail of Friends)*

As the founder of the Paws 4 Peace program at Full Circle Restorative Justice, I was honored and excited to share this compassionate connection with animals and healing approach with Victims and Offenders. At the 2017 National Association of Community and Restorative Justice conference in Oakland, CA (NACRJ), two dear volunteers and their therapy dog drove from Colorado to assist in introducing this new inter-species collaboration for peace. Greg and Ruth Phillips related their Circle experiences while showcasing Abby, in addition to spotlighting FCRJ's "powerhouse" of volunteer facilitators and therapy dog teams.

When asked to explain how this concept of a cross-collaboration of the species in a social justice initiative evolved, my response is deceptively simple: "It just made sense." Being an 'Animal Person', and one who regards our fellow creatures on this planet as sentient beings who connect with humans on many levels, (in addition to having enhanced my life with canine companions for decades), I've always had a strong belief in the 'Power of Paws'.

It seems probable that my background in journalism, and my work with animal companions as a professional pet sitter with *Angel of the Animals* influenced my creative thought process in launching the Paws 4 Peace program. *"The Human-Animal Bond Online"* was the focus of my graduate thesis for the School of Journalism and Mass Communications at the University of Colorado in Boulder back in 1997.

Do a search online and you'll find numerous scientific studies providing evidence which touts the benefits of human-animal bonding, and these studies are becoming increasingly common. The recent popularity of "Emotional Support" animals appears to support this trend as well.

In the article *How Dogs Help People Get Along Better* by Jill Suttie (March 6, 2017), she references a study by Central Michigan University which suggests that *"when dogs are around, groups are closer, more cooperative, and more trusting."*

The study's lead author, Steve Colarelli goes on to say:

"...results suggest that there is something about the presence of a dog that increases kind and helpful behavior in groups. When people work in teams, the presence of a dog seems to act as a social lubricant. Dogs seem to be beneficial to the social interactions of teams."

In the summer of 2016, I was seated next to a gentleman with a white, fluffy Golden Retriever wearing a red therapy dog vest on the deck of a local restaurant in scenic Salida, Colorado. Gary and Dolores were approachable, and he was willing to answer my questions regarding therapy dogs. When his wife Terry arrived, I was expressing my interest in recruiting therapy dogs for V-O conferences, and she shared with me her experience as an investigator for the Public Defender's Office. This seemed to be a natural fit, and I asked if she and Dolores would be willing to volunteer in a brand new capacity for our local RJ program as the therapy dog team in V-O conferences.

Soon after I had the great fortune of meeting Greg and Ruth Phillips while conducting a Non-Violent Communication (NVC) weekend workshop in Salida, in October 2016. One of the break-out sessions was on Restorative Justice. Long-time retired educators, both Greg and Ruth are also therapy dog handlers who developed a strong interest in RJ. When they shared with me that their Border Collie Abby was actively volunteering as a therapy dog, I was thrilled at this fortuitous meeting!

The Therapy Dog Teams in RJ consists of (obviously) the therapy dog - and his/her handler, **who has been trained as an RJ facilitator**. By the time FCRJ began implementing the Paws 4 Peace program, Terry and Dolores, and Ruth and Greg with Abby, had joined FCRJ as fully trained Teams, each with the intention of volunteering to facilitate in the Circles.

Together with Jessica Ervin, then FCRJ program coordinator, we then became the founding pack members of Paws 4 Peace!

Chapter 3

RJ: Going to the Dogs

> *"The world would be a nicer place if everyone had the ability to love unconditionally as a dog."* - M.K. Clinton, (Author)
>
> ***

"Recently, I was invited to bring my therapy dog, Abby, to a Full Circle Restorative Justice (FCRJ) V-O conference.

One purpose of FCRJ is to bring parties together who are involved in some type of a dispute and facilitate a resolution that addresses the issues and repairs the harm done. Since nerves are on edge and stress levels are high, the presence of a therapy dog can bring a calming, nonjudgmental presence to the proceedings.

The Circle I attended involved a crime committed by a young offender. FCRJ enabled the victims of this crime and the offender to sit together and work out a resolution satisfactory to all parties.

The transformation on both sides from fear and anger to the honest realization of the impact the offender's choices had on the victims and the community was made through heartfelt communication and the support from everyone there. A written contract was made with recommendations and agreed upon by all present. With continued support from the victim, FCRJ and the family, this young offender will be kept out of the court system.

I truly am grateful that I had the opportunity to be a part of this meeting and hope to be involved in many more. I encourage everyone to learn more and support FCRJ. It is my hope that the court system will continue to refer young offenders to Full Circle Restorative Justice. It has proven to be an extremely effective approach for the healing of both parties involved and has been shown to greatly reduce repeat offenses. As for Abby, she played her role beautifully as only a therapy dog can."

*Ruth Phillips, FCRJ Facilitator and Therapy Dog Handler
in a Letter to the Editor, The Mountain Mail, Salida, Colorado, July 18, 2017*

Therapy Dogs in the Restorative Circle/Conference Process

Many RJ participants experience RJ processes as uniquely transformational, bringing healing and closure to a difficult period in the lives of those affected. Well-trained therapy dogs serve to enhance the initial meeting and assessment of the potential participants in the pre-conference,, and then they are there to soothe the members of victim-offender circle/conferences.

"It is amazing how much love and laughter they [dogs] bring into our lives and even how much closer we become with each other because of them." — John Grogan (Author, Marley & Me)

At the Colorado State RJ Conference, Vail, September 2016
Dolores, Terry & Gary Bolte, Patty LaTaille,
Greg & Ruth Phillips, and Abby

The RJ process needs to be extremely well-regulated and best practices are followed to ensure a successful resolution experience for all. To ensure the best possible outcome, directors and facilitators of RJ programs need to vett their volunteer therapy dog teams very carefully.

Well-regulated and best practices are followed to ensure a successful resolution experience for all. To ensure the best possible outcome, directors and facilitators of RJ programs need to vett their volunteer therapy dog teams very carefully.

Basic behaviors are required before a team is considered for training to participate in a Circle:

Therapy Dogs Requirements

- The dog must be well trained and easily controlled
- The dog must look to their handler for direction.
- The dog and handler must be able to interact well with everyone they encounter including other dogs.
- The dog must feel comfortable with strangers petting them. Small dogs must feel comfortable with strangers picking up and holding them.
- The dogs must be well groomed at all times.
- The dog must show no signs of aggression - i.e., growling, snarling, or showing of teeth.

So why bring dogs into RJ? Therapy dogs serve to soothe and comfort individuals in stressful and anxiety-producing situations, they serve as psychological as well as physiological healers.

Therapeutic Benefits of Therapy Dogs:

Physical:
- Releases calming endorphins
- Lowers blood pressure
- Increases cardiovascular health

Mental:
- Lowers anxiety
- Provides comfort
- Lifts spirits and lessens depression
- Encourages communication
- Increases socialization
- Decreases feelings of alienation and isolation
- Illustrative of the Human-Animal Bond

Since the idea and use of a therapy dog team is new in RJ practices, we've experienced some challenges in the implementation phase of introducing dogs in Circles. It was trial by success and error, or in other words, on the job training (OJT) for all concerned.

In selecting a particular therapy dog team for each Circle, our decision is based on the Team's personalities and experience which is best suited for the individual cases, similar to the process of selecting specific facilitators and community members.

Some of the positive effects we have discovered by including therapy dogs in RJ circles are:

- Calms initial unease, anxiety, & tension
- Enhances communication and connection
- Promotes a positive influence on social/RJ interactions
- "Decompression time" - at the end of a Circle - is more interactive.

At the end of a Circle, healthy snacks are available and participants generally eat and interact after they complete their written evaluation surveys. The 'magic' generally happens here, with sincere conversations, apologies and hugs evolving organically between the victims and offenders. Having a therapy dog interact with people either by giving treats, belly rubs or even playing ball enhances the sweetness of the connections.

"During a Circle, a mother and son were experiencing major anxiety. Due to therapeutic presence of Abby, this anxiety was reduced. She also worked her magic with the victim. Filled with anger toward the offender and doubt about the RJ process, the victim felt that having Abby by her side calmed her nerves and reduced her anger. When the circle ended, she shared what a calming influence Abby's presence had, and felt that having her by her side allowed her to communicate in an honest, open, less confrontational manner. Obviously, the impact dogs have in circles will vary. Yet when the connection is made with the offender or victim and the dog, it is truly magical!"

Shared by Ruth Phillips, with Abby – RJ Therapy Dog Team

Decompression time: Patty and Rosie relaxing
after a Circle; Bailey, Colorado 2018

Here's what FCRJ staff & volunteers have discovered in the three year period of providing therapy dogs in Victim Offender Dialogues, Non Violent Communication, and Peer Mediation school programs, in addition to Facilitator trainings and other events.

Paws 4 Peace Best Practices:

- All participants must be alerted to the potential presence of a therapy dog in the RJ process and agree to sign a waiver.*

- The handler must be trained and certified as an RJ facilitator.

- The Teams must provide proof of therapy dog certification and liability insurance.

- The Team attends the pre-conferences in addition to the Circles.

- The Team will meet and greet participants at the door or entrance to the building and escort them to the conference room.

- The handler's first priority is to minimize distractions and monitor the dogs' behavior. If there are negative interactions, the Team will excuse themselves from the Circle.

- The handler will introduce her/himself and the dog and speak to their role in the Conference. (An example is provided below.)

- The Team will be seated next to the Victim's support members.

- The Team will closely monitor the dialogue and maneuver the Dog to the individuals either speaking and/or needing emotional support.

- Small dogs may be held and/or passed around the Circle if requested.

- The Handler will interact in the role of a Community member.

- During the process of an Agreement/Contract, the dog may be released to rest in the middle of the Circle (Dog beds are always welcome.)

- Dog treats may be provided during the Decompression sharing snacks/breaking bread phase at the end of the Circle.

The concept of having a therapy dog in an RJ program needs to be introduced either in person, in Court and in the initial Welcome Letter to both the Victim and Offender. One example is:

"This program will be teaming up with a Pet Therapy dog and handler to assist in providing a safe and comforting environment for all participants in the Restorative Circle. Please alert the Program Director in advance if you have any concerns or allergies to dogs."

The Therapy Dog Team selected has the dog serving as a comfort animal, and the handler in the role of a community member. In the pre-conference, introductions are made by the facilitator and co-facilitator, and the Team explains their role in the RJ process. An example is:

My name is Ruth, and this is Abby. Abby is a certified therapy dog. Since the experience of participating in a restorative justice can involve stress and tension, Abby is here to help relieve that stress. The experience of having a dog by your side that you can make physical contact with has been proven helpful in a stressful situation. She often responds to that need on her own, but if she doesn't, I encourage you to ask for her, and I'll bring her to you."

At the conclusion of the pre-conference and the determination that the individual met the criteria as a candidate for RJ*, the Team will reassure the participants that the Dog and Handler will be looking forward to seeing them again in the actual Circle. Reconnecting with the dog, and knowing that the Team will be a welcoming presence in the Circle, serves to reduce anxiety regarding the upcoming event.

In the Circle, the Team will be seated in a community member position next to the Victim and support persons. This positioning ensures direct access and closeness to the Victim. A clean, presentable and odor-free dog bed may be placed in the center of the Circle.

---

* HB 1032: The first major restorative justice bill in Colorado established the availability of restorative justice for juveniles, adults, offenders in DOC, DYC and in schools. Should victims request RJ, appropriate offenders are those who 1. accept responsibility for their offenses and 2. are willing to repair the harm 3. voluntarily meet face-to-face with victims, community members and a trained facilitator.

Depending on the Team and the space available in the conference room, the Handler may walk the Dog around the outside of the Circle to be positioned next to the Offender who initially speaks. Then the dog is moved to the Victim who is next to speak. Finally, the dog may be walked to participants who appear to need or ask for comfort and support. A small Dog may be picked up and passed throughout the Circle to settle on the lap of the person who requests/needs canine comfort.

Alternatively, the leash may be passed one by one to each of the participants who request the Dog's soothing presence, while the Handler monitors the progression. The Lead and/or Co-Facilitator may indicate with a look, or unobtrusive head nod to the Handler, if they see a need for the Dog to be positioned differently. Ultimately, it is the handler's responsibility to monitor the dog's behavior and properly position the dog in the Circle.

Patty LaTaille

FCRJ Board President Zech Papp and Dolores in a mock Circle with facilitators Forrest Whitman, Andy Dungan, and Judy Dockery, 2016

Regarding Therapy Dog Positioning:
What to look for as a Facilitator regarding Dog/Handler positioning

- A simple request for the Dog's presence from an individual.

- An emotional moment that the Dog may sense and in some instances intuitively knows to head towards the individual in distress.

- As an expression of empathy after the participant has been heard and his/her contribution to the dialogue validated.

- When the initial dialogue has transitioned to developing an Agreement/Contract to repair the harm, the Dog may settle down to sleep either in the middle of the Circle or by the individual he/she chooses (usually the Handler).

When the Circle is completed, the Dog may be released from being "on duty" and can interact casually and even play with the participants during "Decompression & Snack Time".

"I don't pretend to understand the spiritual connection that is present in each encounter, yet I can tell you that I'm blessed by observing Dolores' interactions with each person she encounters. As it relates to the RJ process, a Circle comes to mind that was very difficult.

A teenage boy had basically shut down emotionally during the Circle and Dolores kept nudging his arm to get him to engage with her. The boy did not want to touch Dolores, but at the end of the Circle, he began playing with her and petting her. Dolores stayed near him and before the process was completed, he was smiling, and enjoying her trick. That experience reconfirmed the powerful human animal bond that is available for us to embrace and be enriched by."

~ Insight shared by Terry Bolte, FCRJ Therapy Dog Team.

Chapter 4

Therapy Dogs and. Service Dogs

> *"Dogs don't rationalize. They don't hold anything against a person. They don't see the outside of a human, but the inside of a human."*
> *"The Dog Whisperer" Cesar Millan, (Mexican American Dog Behaviorist)*

Service dogs are dogs that assist their physically and or/emotionally disabled owners, and are trained by professionals. These dogs perform tasks and then do the work that eases their handler's disabilities. They work with their disabled owners as part of a team. Service dogs give their owners a sense of safety and independence. They are not meant to be petted or interacted with by anyone other than their owners. This is very important to remember, because petting or distracting service dogs may prevent them from performing their job correctly. Most service dogs will be wearing a vest indicating that they are working and are not meant to be petted or interacted with.

The Americans With Disabilities Act (ADA) allows people with disabilities to take their service dogs with them in public places such as hotels, restaurants, grocery stores, etc. Other initiatives such as Transportations Air Carrier Access Act, The Housing and Urban Development Fair Housing Act, and the Federal Rehabilitation Act allow people with disabilities to have their animals with them in many circumstances under which the ADA may not apply.

Therapy dogs are also well trained, yet for a very different purpose. These dogs visit individuals who are in need of comfort, support and/or stimulation, with their handlers acting in a volunteer capacity. They are responsible to provide emotional, psychological, or physiological therapy to people, in addition to their handlers. Therapy dogs must have extremely friendly, stable and easy-going personalities. They are used in many different ways, including visits to schools, libraries, nursing homes, hospices, restorative justice circles and in a variety of other venues. They are meant to be petted and handled, and are encouraged to interact with a variety of people.

Quite often, these dogs are used in psychotherapy practices, physical rehabilitation therapy, and various programs, such as ones that give children the confidence to read out loud. Therapy dogs do not judge.

These special canines are also present in Restorative Justice programs to ease tensions in facilitated Circles, and also in courtroom settings to provide comfort to victims of crime or violence, especially with children.

Therapy dogs can be trained by their owners, yet they must meet set standards and pass a certification test in order to be registered and allowed to participate in therapy dog activities. Please note that therapy dogs are **not** allowed the same public access rights that are granted by law to service dogs. They are not allowed on airplanes, or in stores, restaurants, and other public buildings without specific approval by those entities. This is because the handler does not have a disability that the dog is individually trained to mitigate.

Therapy Dog Team Basic Requirements

Numerous therapy dog training organizations exist throughout the United States and globally. They can be accessed by viewing a "Google" search on the internet at "Therapy Dog Organizations in ...". A brief sample list of therapy dog organizations and their affiliates in Colorado includes the following:

K9c.a.r.e.s. (Westminster, CO) www.prweb.com
www.faithfully k9.com

Denver Pet Partners (Littleton, CO) www.denverpetpartners.org

American Kennel Club "AKC" (50 States) www.akc.org

Pet Partners (50 States) www.petpartners.org

Therapy Dogs of Boulder County (Boulder, CO)
www.therapydogsofbouldercounty.com

Animals 4 Therapy (Golden, CO)
www.animals4therapy.org

Alliance of Therapy Dogs:
www.therapydogs.com

Therapy Dogs International:
www.tdi-dog.org

Paula Barclay

General Requirements for Therapy Dog Team Certification or Registration:

Any breed or mixed breed of dogs, aged one year or older may be tested with a handler to become a registered therapy dog. Typically wolves, wolf-hybrids or coyotes, and coyote-hybrids cannot be registered as therapy dogs because the required rabies vaccination has not been proven effective in these animals.

Most therapy dog training organizations require proof of vaccinations and a yearly fecal exam. All dogs should be deemed in good health by a veterinarian.

Specific Requirements:

- Handlers must demonstrate the ability to give cues and commands to their dogs clearly and quietly, and should correct their dog's inappropriate behavior (jumping/barking) quickly and quietly as well.

- Handlers should remain calm and in control of their dog at all times.

- Dogs should look to handler for direction.

- Both dog and handler must demonstrate that they interact well with every person they encounter. The dog must demonstrate that he/she is friendly to strangers and socially interacts well with humans and other dogs. Handlers must ensure that their dog remains at least 2 feet away from any other dogs to avoid interaction or playing between the dogs.

- The dogs must demonstrate that they are comfortable being touched and stroked on their head, (including the ears), body and tail by a stranger. A small dog must be comfortable being picked up and held in the arms of a stranger.

- During the evaluation and testing process, a therapy team will be dismissed if the handler uses excessive discipline or inappropriate treatment of the dog. A dog may be dismissed from the program for growling, excessive barking, and unfriendly, shy or aggressive behavior.

- Therapy dogs should be well groomed at all times and wear appropriate registration "vests" or identification disclosing their affiliated therapy dog organization.

- A series of at least 3 observations are conducted with the dog and handler by a certified tester. At least two of the observations must be conducted in a medical facility, such as a hospital or nursing home.

Highly trained therapy dogs provide multiple opportunities for excellent public relations for Restorative Justice organizations, victim advocate programs, court room proceedings and other agencies. Local media are usually happy to provide full coverage for well-trained therapy dogs participating in or with dog programs that enhance the human animal bond in community programs and events. When therapy dogs attend fund raising events, more potential donors are apt to attend. The benefits of using certified therapy dogs covered by liability insurance in RJ programs and Circles include providing emotional support for offenders, victims, their families and community members.

For either Service or Therapy dogs, however, the benefits they bring to us are immeasurable. The comfort, unconditional love, and companionship that a dog offers brings us peace, stability, and a sense of equanimity that is unmatched!

Perhaps it will become clearer if we let one of the dogs "speak" as a representative:

Hi, my name is Abby, and I'm a certified therapy dog. I'm also a Border Collie. In many people's minds Border Collie and therapy dog just don't mix. After all, Border Collies are known for their high energy, workaholic attitude. Now don't misunderstand me. I take my jobs very seriously. A job is not worth doing, unless it is done right! What makes me unique is, I just love people, especially kids! I believe human beings were put on this Earth just to give me attention! So, you might say I was born with a very special talent to love and be loved by people.

My mom and dad discovered this special gift I have when I was quite young. They took me to a local trainer who explained what my job would be as a therapy dog. I had to prove that I was able to behave myself in a variety of situations. Once I did that, I registered with an organization called Alliance of Therapy Dogs. I even have my own vest and a business card! Now I get to go into nursing homes and hospitals.

I watch with pride as I see the smiles appear on people's faces that normally don't have much to smile about. I've also heard some amazing stories when I go into elementary schools. The kids love to read to me!

One of my favorite jobs is when I'm part of a restorative justice circle. Since dogs are very sensitive to the energy that people give off, I usually sense some fear, tension and a lot of anxiety! But I've come to help these people. I'm not sure what I do exactly, but when these people see me, the energy shifts and they are able to smile and relax, at least just a little.

One circle I remember the most was the very first one I was invited to. A young man did something he wasn't supposed to. He and his mom were really, really nervous! My mom told me later that they both had something called an anxiety disorder. I have no idea what that is, but I didn't care. I was there to share the love, and I did. I just sat between them and enjoyed their petting! In that same circle I sat next to a lady who was very angry about something that happened to her. Allowing her to pet me seemed to help her, too! It worked like magic! Maybe it's the feeling of my fur. It is pretty silky, after all.

It's a difficult job being a therapy dog, but some lucky dogs get to do it!

Abby Phillips: Ready to work, 2016

Chapter 5

Meet ourTherapy Dog Teams

"I've always had this feeling," Henry says, "that all dogs are really therapy dogs." Meg Donohue, Author of Dog Crazy: A novel of Love Lost and Found

The Paws 4 Peace program in Full Circle Restorative Justice has been operating since 2016 with proven results and a high level of satisfaction by victims and offenders, as well as with the other circle participants. The number of therapy dog teams has grown to six, with many dogs in waiting for FCRJ's annual facilitator training.

I am honored to introduce FCRJ's pioneering teams of amazing canine companions and compassionate humans.

Terry and Dolores

Terry Bolte and "Dolores" Therapy Dog Team

Terry is a retired criminal investigator, employed for 18 years with the State of Colorado. She worked in the financial crimes unit of the Colorado State Securities Division, within the Colorado Department of Regulatory Agencies. Terry's employment experience includes investigations of securities fraud, theft against elderly at risk adults and money laundering. Terry is familiar with confidentiality requirements, court room protocol and has working knowledge of the criminal justice system. In 2015, Terry completed facilitator training with Full Circle Restorative Justice in Salida, Colorado.

Dolores is a 7 year old Golden Retriever. She initially started her training as a service dog through Canine Partners of the Rockies (a service dog organization). At 8 months old, Dolores was diagnosed with a genetic growth issue in her right leg deeming her unable to withstand the 24/7 requirements of a service dog. She was released from that program and changed her career to therapy work. Terry and Dolores are registered as a therapy dog team through Alliance of Therapy Dogs Inc. and are also members of the Chaffee County Therapy Dog organization.

As a registered therapy team, they participate in continuing education and training to maintain and increase their skills and knowledge of how best to serve the community in a fashion that brings comfort, reduces anxiety and eases stress. They visit patients and staff at Heart of the Rockies Regional Medical Center in Salida, Colorado on a weekly basis. They have also visited schools, nursing homes and hospice patients in South Dakota and Colorado.

Dolores and Terry are involved in the FCRJ program, participating in restorative circles to ease stress and encourage a calm, caring environment for both the victim and offenders involved in the restorative justice process of each case.

Dolores truly loves her "job". She is a "toucher" - meaning that she loves to touch people with her paws. She is a gentle soul that loves life, people and treats!

Greg and Ruth Phillips and "Abby" Therapy Dog Team:

Greg and Ruth are both retired after teaching at the elementary level for 30 years. They became involved with Full Circle Restorative Justice after the executive director discovered they owned a certified therapy dog. After being involved with a few Circles and witnessing the positive impact the process can have on both the victim and the offender, they decided to become facilitators. Through FCRJ, Greg and Ruth have also been trained as facilitators of the Insight Prison Project that was developed at San Quentin Prison in California. They are currently facilitating groups at the Buena Vista Correctional Facility in Colorado.

Abby is a 9 year old Border Collie who absolutely adores people, especially kids. It is because of this connection she has with people that inspired Greg and Ruth complete her certification as a therapy dog. She received her certification from the Alliance of Therapy Dogs and is also a member of the Chaffee County Therapy Dogs organization. Abby puts smiles on the residents faces at the nursing home, reads with elementary children, and calms nerves during restorative justice circles. She enjoys competing in agility trials, loves to hike, and sees everyone as a playmate when it comes to playing ball.

Greg and Ruth with Abby

Patty LaTaille and "Kharmalita" Therapy Dog Team:

Patty LaTaille's background in Restorative Justice as a facilitator and her familiarity with canine companions led to the creation of the Paws 4 Peace program while she was in the position of executive director for Full Circle Restorative Justice. Patty's professional background revolves around Social Justice and Communications in various venues. She is the Lead Facilitator and Trainer for Victim-Offender conferencing, as well as serving as a Professional Mediator with Keeping The Peace, LLC. She is the Humanizing Justice Systems and Social Media Lead on the Cornerstone Leadership Council for The Peace Alliance.

Kharmalita made her debut as FCRJ's mascot and docile office dog in 2014 and was the reserve dog available for enhancing communication and connection until 2017. She initially stood in as a therapy dog for a Circle with two young girls who adored dogs, and were very upset when they were informed that neither Dolores or Abby were available.

Kharmie's first job was to lie quietly on her bed in the middle of a Circle and the participants would pet her as needed. She then passed her Therapy Dog certification with flying colors and was deemed a "natural". Kharmie the

Dachshund – Mexican Beach Dog mix has now worked her magic in many RJ Circles, with patients in hospitals, residents of nursing homes and those in Hospice care in Colorado, Long Island, New York and San Miguel de Allende, Mexico. She is a well-traveled, well-pampered and the sweetest 13-year old mixed breed fur baby.

Patty and Kharmie

Patrick Alexander Rudback

Sue Armijo and "Ringo" Therapy Dog Team

Sue, an elementary teacher for 30 years in her "past" life enjoys traveling the globe exploring other cultures. Sue and her husband Roger help raise service dogs for people with mobility issues. She loves to read, hike, and experience the great outdoors. "I really enjoy volunteering with Ringo. He brings a lot of joy to all!", shares smiling Sue.

Ringo, a 6 year old Golden Retriever loves to volunteer at the hospital and the local elementary school in Salida, Colorado. Ringo was rescued when his owner died; they had been an active Therapy Dog team. Sue adopted Ringo after her therapy dog died unexpectedly. Together they created a new team. Ringo enjoys hiking and playing with other dogs. He also loves his frozen vegetables!

Sue and Ringo

Debby Gower and "Rosie" and "Emmy" Therapy Dog Team

Debby has been involved with showing, training, raising, and sharing her golden retrievers for over 35 years. She has also participated in pet therapy for over 18 years. Debby and her dogs were members of Therapy Pet Pals for 16 years. They visited nursing facilities and the VA Outpatient Facility in Austin, Texas.

Debby was awarded Therapy Pet Pal of the Year after two years of working with Pet Pals. In 2016, she moved to Howard, Colorado, and became members of Alliance Of Therapy Dogs. They are also members of the Chaffee County Therapy Dog Organization.

Rosie is a 10 1/2 year old golden retriever who has been a Registered Therapy Dog for 9 years. She currently visits the Heart of the Rockies Medical Center every Tuesday. Their Team completed the FCRJ Facilitator Training in May 2017. Debby calls Rosie her "Velcro Girl", because she always has to be touching the person who is petting her.

Emmy is a 6 1/2 year old golden retriever who has been a Registered Therapy Dog for five years. She currently visits Star Point weekly in Salida, Colorado. Star Point is a program for adults with cognitive and physical challenges.

Rosie and Emmy take part in FCRJ to help Circle members settle in, stay calm, and ease any tensions that might occur. The dogs have an uncanny ability to sense when they are needed.

Debby, Rosie and Emmy

Paula Barclay and "Keet" Therapy Dog Team

Keet joined the lives of her owners in a rather unique way. Paula and partner Bryan Lally were on a back country hike to a remote Anasazi ruin in Navajo National Monument in 2014. Soon after they left their car near Kayenta, Arizona, a scruffy young dog began following them. They tried to shoo it away, but the dog persisted. That dog became known as Keet, because she ended up following them for two days during their 20-mile round trip hike to the cliff dwelling, Keet Seel. When Paula and Bryan got back to their car, still with the dog in tow, they decided to take her home, clean her up, and find a good home for her. "We are foster failures," relates Bryan, laughing.

Once home, they discovered what a unique and special dog Keet actually is. She is naturally fun-loving, confident and happy, but she's also calm and loving, and seems to have an innate sense of what people want. Paula and Bryan realized that her personality made her well-suited to therapy dog work.

Keet and Paula love working with team members at Full Circle Restorative Justice. "I think Keet does great. She knows when to stay out of the way and when someone needs some quiet support," says Paula. "FCRJ and the Paws 4 Peace Program plays such an important and special role in our community. We are proud to be a part of such a positive force for change."

As well as being a Therapy Dog Team with FCRJ, Keet and Paula participate in the "Paws for Reading" program at Longfellow Elementary, and also provide comfort at the Heart of the Rockies hospital, both located in Salida, Colorado.

When Keet's not volunteering in the community, she loves to go fishing with Bryan, hiking in the woods, and learning new tricks on the agility course.

Keet, Paula, and Bryan hiking in the Colorado Rockies 2017

Paws 4 Peace in the news…

Paws for Peace

by Patty LaTaille
Loyal Duke's Columnist

Loyal Duke's Scoop

Restorative Justice (RJ) is a commonsense approach to dealing with incidences of crime and/or conflict.

Those who were impacted – the individual(s) who caused the harm (offender) and the person(s) impacted by the harm (victim) – and their family/support people meet face to face with trained facilitators who initiate dialogue in a Restorative Circle.

These circles are supported by community members – and now Therapy Dog Teams – who assist in holding those who caused the harm accountable, while developing an agreement on how to make it right.

The trained RJ facilitator/handler and nationally certified therapy dogs promote the RJ focus on the "back story," its compassionate approach of respecting all participants equally and providing closure and the means to repair the harm, leading to healing for victims, offenders and community.

Here in Chaffee County and the 11th Judicial District we are fortunate to have Full Circle Restorative Justice (FCRJ) collaborating with the courts, schools and community to address harm done and helping repair relationships.

As an experienced RJ facilitator, I noted the uncomfortable moments when the victim and offender initially sat down in a Restorative Circle

together. How to ease the inherent tension? We needed an "ice breaker" to assist in creating connection and building rapport.

Who better to do this than a dog – a cute canine connector who helps meet individual needs for ease and comfort? This pioneering approach evolved into FCRJ's Paws for Peace program– therapy dogs are now welcomed into the victim-offender conferencing process.

By inviting a certified therapy dog into the circle/conference, RJ practitioners take concrete steps to ease the tension and to calm anxiety experienced by participants. Therapy Dog Teams provide comfort and connection throughout this extremely effective and transformational process known as restorative justice. Find out more at fullcirclerj.org.

Patty LaTaille is one of the founding members and current program director of Full Circle Restorative Justice. She shares her life with Kharmalita, the Full Circle mascot and certified therapy dog, who she said has taught her the healing power of the dog.

August 24, 2018

Full Circle Restorative Justice attends national conference

by **Guinne Stropes**
Mail Intern

Patty LaTaille and Molly Leach of Full Circle Restorative Justice said they experienced true cross-cultural representation at a conference for the National Association for Communities and Restorative Justice June 16-18 in Oakland, Calif.

Americans of African and Native American descent were fully and equally represented, LaTaille said.

Full Circle's presentation at the event highlighted the benefits of using therapy dogs in the restorative justice process.

Ruth and Greg Phillips, Salida, whose therapy dog, Abby, works with the Full Circle Restorative Justice program in Salida, drove to California with Abby to attend the conference.

"Abby was the only dog attending," said LaTaille. "She wore her vest, and her job was to greet people and get petted. She was the star of the conference — a real celebrity."

About 1,200 people attended the biannual conference, the sixth of its kind. The Full Circle presenters were given a "prime time" slot because of the pioneering nature of their program in the ways of interspecies collaboration, said LaTaille. Approximately 60 people attended their presentation.

Full Circle's pioneering approaches were well received with the main question being, "How did you come up with this idea (to use therapy dogs in restorative justice)," said LaTaille. Other questions included inquiries about the "Paws for Peace" T-shirts the group was wearing.

Courtesy photo
From left, Patty LaTaille, executive director of Full Circle Restorative Justice, and Ruth and Greg Phillips, all of Salida, kneel next to Abby the therapy dog before presenting at the 2017 National Association for Community and Restorative Justice conference in Oakland, Calif. Full Circle's presentation focused on interspecies collaboration, especially using therapy dogs in the restorative justice practice because of their adeptness at calming people in stressful situations.

"When people asked where we came up with the idea, I told them it arose from my thesis paper, which focused on interspecies relations. It was written when I was graduating with my journalism and mass communications degree," she said.

"Because we had nearly 30 or 40 people asking us if we were selling the shirts, we've decided to offer them online at fullcirclerj.net," said LaTaille. "We will be taking pre-orders as soon as we get the image and purchase order form online in a day or so."

LaTaille said because there were so many cultures represented, she experienced being in a minority group. "We got to see restorative justice through a racial equity lens. All the presentations were informative, yet I really enjoyed a main conference speaker's presentation about restorative justice and its indigenous roots," she said.

"Overall, the conference went very well, and people were enthused about Full Circle's presentation. Most people there had canine companions and many of the restorative justice groups mentioned that they would begin searching for registered therapy dogs to join their restorative justice programs," said LaTaille.

About the Author:

Ms. LaTaille (Patty) is currently the Program Director of Full Circle Restorative Justice (FCRJ), founded in 2006 and based in Salida, Colorado. Her professional background revolves around Social Justice and Communications in various venues. She is an international speaker on methods of Non Violent Communication (NVC).

In addition to acting as the Lead Facilitator and Trainer for Victim-Offender conferencing in FCRJ, Patty practices as a Professional Mediator with *Keeping The Peace, LLC*. She also serves as the Humanizing Justice Systems and Social Media Lead on the Cornerstone Leadership Council for *The Peace Alliance*.

After earning a graduate degree in Journalism and Mass Communications from the University of Colorado at Boulder, Patty was employed by IBM in Boulder, CO, as a Communications Architect. At the same time, she started *Angel of the Animals*, a pet sitting service which served Boulder and Salida, CO. Patty has a number of published works and photos in corporate and media publications, regional newspapers and magazines, and in *Chicken Soup for the Working Woman's Soul*.

Diego Rojas Lopez

pattylataille · Follow

pattylataille Paws 🐾 for Peace book in progress!

aussie_vegan_grandma I am soooooooo excited that you are writing the book. FINALLY 🏆🏆🏆🏆 You would not believe the RC work we are now doing in local schools and CJ is part of it. I tell them about you all the time. so we need you back for a visit so that the students can hang with you. Love you my Soul Sista 💗 💗 💗

pattylataille I FINALLY took a break from trying to save the world 😊 So yes - thank you for your support!! 😊 And can't wait to hear more about your work & darling CJ's role!! 💗 🐾 I will come back during my book promotion tour! 👍 😊

pattylataille 💗 💗 💗 YOU!!

♡ ○ ⬆

21 likes

FEBRUARY 18, 2018

36

Patty enjoys spending active time outdoors and with young people & animals. In prior years, she worked and played at being a ski/snowboard instructor and a white water river guide. She has more than twenty five years of experience in working with and mentoring high-risk adolescents, in addition to founding and managing a number of sustainable youth programs along the way.

Patty originally hails from Long Island, New York and has made her home in the Colorado mountains for 26 years now. She resides there with her furry family members and appreciates her "tribe" of small town friends. Patty's passion for justice and the love of animals, dogs especially, contributed to the founding of the P4P program. She finds "awe" in her life by traveling and connecting within other cultures.

Find Patty on Facebook, LinkedIn, fullcirclerj.org, and keepingthepeacemediation.com

***

"There's nowhere you can be that isn't where you're meant to be, it's easy."
-Lennon and McCartney

A note from Kathleen S. Kennedy at Write With Light Publications:

When I first heard about Paws 4 Peace and the Restorative Justice program, I was enthused and relieved. It is promising practice for our society long in need of ways to repair the ruptures experienced through harmful trauma. The idea of healing deep hurts with the support of our canine friends felt so intuitive, I knew Write With Light Publications was a natural fit to share in the storytelling. Thank you to Patty LaTaille for the collaborative opportunity, to Jeanenne Wagner for bringing us together, and to our furry friends for loving in the most unconditional way possible.

"Everyone thinks they have the best dog. None of them are wrong"
W.R. Purche

"When the dog looks at you, the dog is not thinking what kind of a person you are. The dog is not judging you." Eckhart Tolle (Author, Spiritual Teacher)